There surely could be no greater blessing than bringing a child into this world and then having her grow up to be just like you. Your heart is so full of love for all living things, and you're a friend to everyone you meet. Your nature is so giving; your spirit is as pure as a baby's breath. I couldn't ask for a better daughter than you.

— Donna Fargo

Blue Mountain Arts®
Bestselling Books

By Susan Polis Schutz:
To My Daughter, with Love, on the Important Things in Life
To My Son, with Love
I Love You

100 Things to Always Remember... and One Thing to Never Forget
by Alin Austin

Is It Time to Make a Change?
by Deanna Beisser

Trust in Yourself
by Donna Fargo

To the One Person I Consider to Be My Soul Mate
by D. Pagels

For You, Just Because You're Very Special to Me
by Collin McCarty

Chasing Away the Clouds
by Douglas Pagels

Anthologies:
42 Gifts I'd Like to Give to You
Always Believe in Yourself and Your Dreams
Creeds of Life, Love, & Inspiration
Follow Your Dreams Wherever They Lead You
For You, My Daughter
Friends Are Forever
Friends for Life
I Love You, Mom
I'm Glad You Are My Sister
The Joys and Challenges of Motherhood
The Language of Recovery ...and Living Life One Day at a Time
Life Can Be Hard Sometimes ...but It's Going to Be Okay
Marriage Is a Promise of Love
May You Always Have an Angel by Your Side
Mottos to Live By
Take Each Day One Step at a Time
Teaching and Learning Are Lifelong Journeys
There Is Greatness Within You, My Son
These Are the Gifts I'd Like to Give to You
Think Positive Thoughts Every Day
Thoughts of Friendship
Thoughts to Share with a Wonderful Teenager
To My Child
True Friends Always Remain in Each Other's Heart
With God by Your Side ...You Never Have to Be Alone
Words of Love
You're Just like a Sister to Me

A Daughter
Is Forever

A Blue Mountain Arts® Collection

Featuring Poems by

Susan Polis Schutz
and Donna Fargo

Blue Mountain Press™

SPS Studios, Inc., Boulder, Colorado

Copyright © 2002 by SPS Studios, Inc.

We wish to thank Susan Polis Schutz for permission to reprint the following poems that appear in this publication: "To My Daughter," "I love you every minute…," "I Love Your Beautiful Smile, My Daughter," "To My Daughter, I Love You," "If Ever You Need Someone to Talk to…," "It Is a Wonderful World, My Daughter…," and "Always Believe in Yourself, Daughter." Copyright © 1986, 1988, 1991, 1993, 1996 by Stephen Schutz and Susan Polis Schutz. All rights reserved.

Library of Congress Cataloging-in-Publication Data is available.

ISBN: 0-88396-633-6

ACKNOWLEDGMENTS appear on page 64.

Certain trademarks are used under license.

Manufactured in China
First printing: January 2002

✪ This book is printed on recycled paper.

This book is printed on fine quality, laid embossed, 80 lb. paper. This paper has been specially produced to be acid free (neutral pH) and contains no groundwood or unbleached pulp. It conforms with all the requirements of the American National Standards Institute, Inc., so as to ensure that this book will last and be enjoyed by future generations.

SPS Studios, Inc.

P.O. Box 4549, Boulder, Colorado 80306

Contents

You Are a Wonderful Daughter

I have asked myself
   (as every parent does)
if I have loved you enough
and done the very best job
   that I could for you.
Then, as human nature goes,
   I remember mistakes
      that I made
and how they might have hurt you.
Yet I never stopped loving you,
   even in the times
      when I seemed distant.

I am so proud that you are my child;
when I think of you,
   I feel tears in my eyes
because you make me so happy.
I wonder why I haven't told you this
   much more often than I have,
but sometimes it's hardest to say
   what we feel strongest about.
So I don't want to let
   another moment pass
without telling you
how much you mean to me
and how very much I love you.

— Linda Hersey

Wherever You May Go in Life, Daughter, My Love Goes with You

There are so many things
    I want to say to you,
so many thoughts and feelings
    I want to leave with you,
as you venture out into a world
    of your own making.
I don't know how I can possibly
    express them all.
I want you to know, first of all,
    how much I love you and how proud
        I am of you.
You are, without a doubt, one of the best
    things that has ever happened to me.
Wherever you go in life,
    whatever you choose to do,
I know you'll accomplish greatness.

If you are ever in doubt about anything,
just trust your intuition and go with your
    best judgment, because no one
knows you better than you know yourself.
Don't worry if you make a mistake
    or change your direction from time to time;
you still have many more "learning" years
    ahead of you.
And if you ever need help or advice or
    just someone to talk to,
I'll always be here for you in any way
    that I can be.

Perhaps most important of all,
I want to thank you...
    for all the smiles and good times,
    for the opportunity to share
        your life's experiences,
    for the friendship we now share,
    and for being the best daughter
        anyone could ever ask for.

— Anna Marie Edwards

Dear Daughter of Mine...

Through the years, I watched you grow, change, and constantly question everything. When you were little, there was an overwhelming feeling inside me that wanted to hold you close and keep you safe and warm all your life. Yet as the years passed, I realized that I couldn't do that. You have always been a child full of wonder, and to keep you so close to me would have deprived you of experiencing life's wonders.

Now, after years of letting you go your own way and watching you become a beautiful young lady, our roles have changed. You are still my daughter and I am still your parent, but most precious of all is the fact that we have become good friends, and we have a friendship that will stand the test of time.

I want you to know that I'll always cherish the wonder and joy of watching you grow into a beautiful young lady. I'll always be proud to say, "This is my daughter." But most of all, I'm proud to say that you are my best friend.

— Vicky Lafleur

Daughter, You Are
Such a Blessing to Me

There surely could be no greater blessing than
bringing a child into this world and then having
her grow up to be just like you. Your heart is
so full of love for all living things, and you're a
friend to everyone you meet. Your nature is so
giving; your spirit is as pure as a baby's breath.
I couldn't ask for a better daughter than you.

God blessed me so "good" when you were born
to me. You have never disappointed me in any
way. I know we've had a few ups and downs, but
I wouldn't change you if I could. I love you just
the way you are, and I know you're still changing,
but I also want you to know that I'm proud of the
person you're becoming.

Keep on going in the direction you're going. Keep reaching for your dreams and making them come true. I will always cheer you on and love you.

Today, I want to tell you these things, to show you my unconditional love and acceptance, to tell you how very proud I am of you. I hope each day brings you everything you've ever wanted. You are precious to me beyond words.

Sweet daughter, I wish you the most blessed life. May your guardian angel keep you safe and in the arms of love.

— Donna Fargo

To My Daughter, I Love You

So many times
you ask me questions
and your big beautiful eyes
look at me
with trust, confusion and
innocence
I always hope that my
answers to you
will help guide you
Even though I always want to protect you
and step in for you when you have a
    difficult decision to make
it is very important that I do not interfere
so that you will learn from your own experiences
and develop confidence in your own judgment
There is a fine line between
a mother telling her daughter
too much
or too little
I hope I have struck a proper balance
I have always wanted to tell you
how honored I am that you
seek out my opinions
I appreciate the trust you have in me and
I want you to know that
I have an immense trust in you
I am very proud of you
as I watch you growing up to be an
intelligent, independent, sensitive young woman
I love you

— Susan Polis Schutz

Everything I Do as Your Parent, I Do Out of Love for You

You probably can't imagine the love
    parents have for their children,
But you need to know that it is
    constant and unconditional.
Nothing can change it, and it
    never, ever goes away.
A parent's love is there through the
    discipline and the disagreements;
It's in every action and every decision.
Unfortunately, it isn't always
    apparent or obvious,
And sometimes, parents make mistakes
    or wrong decisions.
We try to do what is best and fair,
    but we don't always get it right.
Emotions, moods, fear, and love
    get in the way.

A fierce desire to keep our children safe
    at all costs
Often causes us to say "no" when
    you are begging for a "yes."
Parents must keep the past and future
    in mind with each choice they make,
Knowing that children often
    see only the "now"
And are not always aware of consequences
    and temptations.
Our goal is to help you become
    all that you can be
So that you are safe and happy now
And can live a fulfilling and successful life
    in the future.
Hopefully, someday you'll understand,
But until then, know that you are a
    special person —
One who is precious, cherished, and —
    most of all —
Loved.

— Barbara Cage

I Love Your Beautiful Smile,
My Daughter

Sometimes I see you
confused
Sometimes I see you
troubled
Sometimes I see you
hurt
and I feel so sad and
helpless
I wish that I could absorb
these feelings from you
and make everything better
but I know that these feelings
will only help you to grow
and understand more about life
These feelings will help you
to become a more sensitive person
So as I watch your eyes
which tell me everything
I will offer you my
understanding and support
I will offer you my
tears and love
I will offer you the
promise that your beautiful
smile will soon return

— Susan Polis Schutz

Wishes for You, Daughter

I wish you love and happiness
Perfect health your whole life through
As much money as you need
    to make life easier
To do the things you want to

I wish you joy and satisfaction
The appreciation you so deserve
Courage when you're fearful
When you're about to lose your nerve

I wish you good friends to call on
A playful heart to keep you young
Special memories to hold on to
Pretty melodies to be sung

I hope you have someone to talk to
And to be with when you please
To share life's special things with
Like a walk among the trees

To share a blanket in the wintertime
To protect you from the cold
To picnic with in the summertime
To hug and kiss and hold

Remember, things may not always work out
    for the best in life
But you can make the best of everything
Just turn those lessons from your journey
Into songs that you can sing

If I could package up my love for you
With a ribbon and a bow
Whatever you want would be yours
    for the asking
Whatever you need, wherever you go

— Donna Fargo

You're a Very Wonderful Daughter

I want you to know of some
special feelings that I carry with me
in my heart all the time.

The feelings are about how much
I cherish you. How proud I am of you.
How many hopes and dreams I want
to come true for you.
    And how happy I want you to be.

Even during some of our heart-to-heart talks,
the words I want to say don't always get said.
But the feelings are always felt.
    Always.

You're a special person... all your own.
    But as you grow and learn and change
        with the days, I want you to know
        of one thing that will never change.

And that... is my endless love... for you.

— Laurel Atherton

As a Daughter,
You Are
This Kind of Beautiful

You have the kind of qualities and characteristics that make people around you glad you're in their world. You have the kind of character that reaches out to others to make the world a better and more beautiful place in which to live. Your beauty is not consumed with its own needs and prejudices but finds satisfaction in giving hope and acceptance and approval to others. It is an internal, soothing kind of beauty that activates the love and appreciation mechanisms in other people, making it easier for everyone to live together. You're this kind of beautiful.

You're the kind of beautiful that doesn't change with the weather or a crisis in life. It is a kind of beauty that provides light in the world for others to use to guide themselves out of difficult circumstances. Although its glow may dim at times when presented with a new challenge, yours is the kind of beauty that will survive the hard places in life, allowing you to learn from them. It will sustain you. You have this kind of beauty.

This kind of beautiful comes from the heart and is powered by a love for others, a desire to be good, to do good, to help and not hurt anyone. It's easy for someone to enhance their appearance on the outside, but to be beautiful inside means reaching out to others with kindness and thoughtfulness and generosity. It is wanting the best for everyone, not just for yourself. It has to do with compassion. That's the way you are. That's the kind of beauty you have.

Being this kind of beautiful allows you to identify with other people's shortcomings in life. This kind of beautiful knows that you must be able to love, forgive, and accept others, or your beauty will lose its essence and its gift, which is the desire to love.

This kind of beauty is soft and easy to be around. It gives more than it takes. It doesn't judge others harshly. It's not egotistical or proud. It doesn't try to change others. It accepts. It shows itself with open arms, not clenched fists; with smiles, not frowns; with joy and laughter, not negativity and reprimands. Being this kind of beautiful is contagious; it lifts others up to accept themselves and to experience their own gift of beauty. Being this kind of beautiful makes others glad to be alive and to know you. You're this kind of beautiful. Thank you for your wonderful example.

— Donna Fargo

If Ever You Need Someone to Talk to, I Am Always Here for You

If ever things are not
going well for you
and you have some problems to solve
If ever you are feeling confused
and don't know the right thing to do
If ever you are feeling frightened
and hurt
or if you just need someone
to talk to
please remember that
I am here for you at all times
without judgment
and with understanding
and love

— Susan Polis Schutz

Family Is the Best Feeling
in the World

The best feeling in this world
  is family.
From it, we draw love,
  friendship, moral support,
and the fulfillment of every
  special need within our hearts.
In a family, we are connected to
  an ever-present source
of sunny moments, smiles and laughter,
understanding and encouragement,
and hugs that help us grow in confidence
  all along life's path.
Wherever we are,
whatever we're doing,
whenever we really need to feel
  especially loved, befriended,
    supported, and cared for
      in the greatest way,
our hearts can turn to the family
and find the very best
  always waiting for us.

— Barbara J. Hall

A Family's Love Can Rise Above Anything That Comes Along

My dear and wonderful daughter,
we all have times
when it seems like
the sun forgot to shine in our lives
and the dreams we were counting
so heavily on... forgot how much
we wanted them to come true.

When you need a place of comfort,
a hand to hold, and a heart that cares
about your happiness more than words
can ever say... remember that you can
turn to me... and I'll do whatever
I can to help you
   chase those clouds away.

— Ann Turrel

Always Believe
in Yourself, Daughter
...and Know that You Are Loved

Know yourself —
what you can do
and want to do in life
Set goals
and work hard to achieve them
Have fun every day in every way
Be creative —
it is an expression
   of your feelings
Be sensitive in viewing the world
Believe in the family
as a stable and rewarding way
of life
Believe in love
as the most complete
and important emotion possible
Believe that you are
an important part of
everyone's life that you touch
Believe in yourself
and know that you are loved

— Susan Polis Schutz

Daughter,
You Are the Light
of My Life

The day you came into my life
a star dropped from the sky
and lit a flame inside my heart
Watching you grow
that light inside my heart burned brighter
fueled by pride in each of your
    accomplishments
and by the greatest love
for all that you have become
This flame keeps me going
It comforts my soul and
    completes my life
knowing that I have blessed the world
with the most precious of gifts

You have made your place in this world
    so quickly
discovering your independence
and becoming your own beautiful person
I want you to know always
that no matter the time that passes
    between us
no matter the distance separating our hearts
my heart will be filled with the light
you sparked so many years ago
and it will continue to burn
so that you will always feel
the love and comfort of home
    and never feel alone

— Deana Marino

You've Earned Your Wings... Fly!

You've earned your wings
The sky's the limit
Go ahead and fly

To the stars
To the moon
Let your dreams take you high

Make your plans
Go all out
Give it all you've got

Don't be afraid
Don't be held back
Courage means a lot

Believe in yourself
Give yourself advice
Just as a friend of yours would

Don't be discouraged
Don't just think about it
Do what you think you should

Let your words and your actions
Be in agreement
Do what you know to do

You've earned your wings
It's just a matter of time now
Until your dreams will come true

— Donna Fargo

It Is a Wonderful World, My Daughter... and You Are a Beautiful Part of It

The world was made
to be beautiful —
but sometimes we get caught up in
everyday actions
completely forgetting about this
completely forgetting that
what is truly important
are the simple, basic things in life —
honest, pure emotions
surrounded by the majestic beauty of nature
We need to concentrate on
the freeness and peacefulness of nature
and not on the driven material aspects of life
We need to smell the clear air
after the rainfall
and appreciate the good in things

Each of us must be responsible
and do our part
in order to help preserve a beautiful world —
the waterfalls, the oceans, the mountains
the large gray boulders
the large green farms
the fluffy pink clouds
the sunrises and sunsets, ladybugs
rainbows, dew, hummingbirds
butterflies, dandelions
We need to remember that
we are here for a short time
and that every day should count for something
and that every day we should be thankful
for all the natural beauty
The world is a wonderful place
and we are so lucky to be a part of it

— Susan Polis Schutz

No Matter Where You Go, Daughter, I Will Always Be Here

A child will grow
And go into the world
As a wonderful person —
Ambitious
Eager to begin the journey
Equipped with knowledge
Endowed with a ready spirit
Educated, bright, and beautiful...
Just as you are

But a parent stays the same —
Always loving you
Always proud of you
Always hoping you know that
A parent is never too far away to listen
Or to care about each moment of your life

Wherever you go
You have my greatest blessing
Be all that you can be
Remembering all the while...
I'm always here for you

— Barbara J. Hall

Daughter, Watching You Grow Up
Has Been My Life's Reward

The happiest moments of my life
Were when you were little and we
      spent our days together.
Watching you take your first step,
Hearing your laughter,
And reading books together
Are memories I will hold in a special place
      in my heart forever.
Sending you off to your first day
      of kindergarten was bittersweet for me.
I knew that growing up was part of life,
And I wanted you to experience
      everything life has to offer,
But I was also sad, because I knew
      that a chapter in my life was closing
And a new page was opening.
I put on a brave face and tried not to cry,
But when I got home, I have to admit,
      I shed some tears.
You were my baby, and you were
      growing up so fast.

As time went on, you grew to be
   a confident young lady.
I watched with joy, and a little nervousness,
   as you went on your first date.
I loved seeing you with your friends.
I was so proud the day you graduated
   from high school
And entered a new phase of your life.
Now you are an adult, and I love you so much.
I am so proud of all that you have become.
I will never be president
And I will probably never be famous,
But I gave birth to you
And helped you grow to be
   the wonderful person you are today.
I feel God's most important job for me
   has been completed.
I have you as my reward.

— Melissa Whitten

When I Look
at You, Daughter…

I see such beauty in the woman you
are becoming, and I'm so glad that you've
stayed close to me. It means so much when
you ask for my advice or opinion on things.
We have a mutual respect for each other
that continues to strengthen. I love to talk
with you about anything… serious or light.
And I love that we can laugh together not
only as parent and child, but as the very
best of friends.

I want you to know how I feel about
you. You have enriched my life more than
you'll ever know, and you have taught me
so much about being a parent, a friend…
and a person. I love you, and I'm so very
proud of you. Please know that no matter
where you may be or where you will go, I'll
be right there with you… in a special place
in your heart.

— debbie peddle

Keep Reaching for the Stars,
Dear Daughter

Day by day, year by year
I've watched you grow
grabbing hold of life
with grace and determination
making it your own
molding your dreams into reality
I've watched you fill to the brim
with happiness and pride
with each new accomplishment
I have seen your heart broken
and felt your pain
as the tears spilled from your eyes
I know the sadness that consumes you
when those who are supposed to care
belittle your ambition
trying to take control
of your destiny

I've seen traces of doubt
begin to invade
tearing at your self-confidence
and I begin to worry
that maybe this time
you won't heal
But after allowing yourself
to feel the pain
to cry the tears
you do heal
Stronger and more determined
you tighten your grip on life
leaving the negative behind
I gladly share all this with you
My daughter
you are a survivor
and you fill me with pride

— Sharon M. McCabe

Daughter,
I'm Proud of the Woman
You Are

When you were young,
I thought of your future life.
Perhaps you would fly to the moon
Or, if not, at least land on a star.
I knew you could do whatever
You set your mind to.
I saw you as a leader,
Strong in your convictions,
Able to move mountains
Not just for yourself,
But for others also.
I am so proud of you,
Of the woman you have become
With all your effort and hard work.
I hope you can feel
The warm love I have for you
Today and always.

— Carol Lawson

Have Some Fun!

Let your hair down
Kick your feet up
Go all out for yourself today

Do something wild
Something unusual
Don't let anyone get in your way

Throw yourself a party
Bake yourself a cake
Do what you want to do

Soak in the joy
Of life's splendor and grandeur
Look in the mirror
  and give thanks for you

Do something different
Get a little crazy
Don't worry about a thing

Pamper yourself generously
Take time for you today
See all the joy you bring

Throw out the schedule
Get rid of the rules
Be as free as a bird in the sky

Let yourself dream big
See yourself "getting there"
Catch a ride on faith and fly high

Roll in the green grass
Act like a little child
Let go of struggle and strife

Pretend it's a holiday
Take time to play today
It's a great day
   to celebrate your life!

— Donna Fargo

May These Endless Gifts
Be Yours Always...

A star to light your way
when you can't see what's ahead.
Strong winds beneath your dreams,
lifting you up and carrying you on.
Prayers, strong and deep,
untying your cares
when the threads get tangled.
Hope in tough situations and
a faith built on God's infinite power.
A harvest of moments, memories,
and good times.
Sunshine amongst the clouds
and smiles that turn anguish to joy.
Silence when words aren't needed.
All that it takes to watch your cares
drift away.
Tomorrows as vast as the universe —
opportunities far beyond
what your heart believes.
Love that is lasting and giving,
a happy life, and a happy heart —
every day, all year.

— Linda E. Knight

A Daughter Is Forever

A daughter is one of the greatest blessings
   one could ever have
She begins her life loving and trusting you
   automatically

For many years, you are the center of her life
Together you experience the delights of
   the new things she learns and does

You enter into a daughter's play and are once
   again young
And even though it's harder to enter into her
   world as she becomes a teen...

You are there, understanding her dilemmas and
   her fears
And wishing with all your heart that she didn't
   have to go through them

A daughter's smile is a precious sight that
   you treasure each time you see it
And the sound of her laughter always brings
   joy to your heart

Her successes mean more to you than your own
And her happiness is your happiness

Her heartaches and disappointments
    become yours, too
Because when she isn't okay, you can't
    be okay either

Daughters aren't perfect
    but you, Daughter, come close to it
You have given me more happiness
    than you know

I am thankful for your kindness and
    thoughtfulness
And I am proud of who you are
    and how you live your life

Words can't express how much you mean to me
    or how much I love you
The love goes too deep, and the gratitude
    and pride I feel are boundless

Thank you for blessing my life
    in so many ways

— Barbara Cage

To My Daughter

My day always becomes wonderful
when I see your
pretty face smiling so sweetly
There is such warmth and intelligence
radiating from you
It seems that every day
you grow smarter and more beautiful
and every day
I am more proud to be your mother
As you go through different stages of life
you should be aware that there will be many times
when you will feel scared and confused
but with your strength and values
you will always end up wiser
and you will have grown from your experiences
understanding more about people and life
I have already gone through
these stages
So if you need advice or someone to talk to
to make sense out of it all
I hope that you will talk to me
as I am continually cheering for your happiness
my sweet daughter
and I love you

— Susan Polis Schutz

Daughter, You Are
Life's Greatest Gift to Me

Memories come flooding back to me
    as I look back over the years.
I want to hold on to you
    and at the same time
watch you fly high and free.

You have such spirit and a character
    all your own.
You are a doer, and an achiever
    of what you believe in.
I'm so proud of your dreams
    and the conviction you have
to make those dreams come true.
Your world is bright, new,
    and bursting with possibilities.

It's so easy to remember
    your very first steps
and how I held out my hand
    for you to hold.
As each year passes,
    you take more steps,
and some of these will eventually
    lead you away from me —
but always remember that my hand
    and my heart are forever here for you.
You will always be my daughter,
    but I have also discovered in you
a rare and precious friend.
You have been life's greatest gift to me,
and I love you so much.

                              — Vickie M. Worsham

My Love for You
Has a Lifetime Guarantee

You are the sparkle in my eyes
and the pride in my heart.
You are the courage that gives me strength
and the love that gives me life.
You are my inspiration
and the best gift I ever received.
Maybe I don't always show it,
but I love you with every beat of my heart.
Maybe I don't always tell you,
but no words can express
    what you mean to me.
I pray that I've always done right by you;
believe me, I've tried my best.
No matter where life's path takes you
or the difficulties you may encounter,
know that I'm with you in spirit.
My love has a lifetime guarantee.
If ever you're in trouble
    or just need a friend,
I'm no further away than a phone call.
You are my child, and I feel so blessed
that I am allowed to be a part of your life.

— Lois Carruthers

I love you every minute of every day, my beautiful daughter

I looked at you today
and saw the same beautiful eyes
that looked at me with love
when you were a baby
I looked at you today
and saw the same beautiful mouth
that made me cry when you first smiled at me
when you were a baby
It was not long ago
that I held you in my arms
long after you fell asleep
and I just kept rocking you
all night long

I looked at you today
and saw my beautiful daughter
no longer a baby
but a beautiful person
with a full range of emotions and feelings
and ideas and goals
Every day is exciting
as I continue to watch you grow
And I want you to always know that
in good and in bad times
I will love you
and that no matter what you do
or how you think
or what you say
you can depend on
my support, guidance
friendship and love
every minute of every day
I love being your mother

— Susan Polis Schutz

Daughter, Here Are Some Things I Want You to Know and Remember...

Please know and remember that it is with the
   greatest joy that I am your guardian, protector,
   and nurturer.
Please know and remember that I will always strive
   to fulfill these roles with honor, trust, and respect
   for your thoughts, feelings, and individuality.
What matters most in life are the people you love,
   and, for always, you will be one of the people
   in my life whom I love the most.
You are the essence of joy and the true meaning
   of life.
You are the part of me that I'm most proud of
   because you're you.
You are a rare and treasured gift.
You are a dream with all its hope and promise.
You are love, endless and pure.
You are my beautiful daughter.
Please know and remember this, always.

— Linda Sackett-Morrison

ACKNOWLEDGMENTS

The following is a partial list of authors whom the publisher especially wishes to thank for permission to reprint their works.

Donna Fargo for "As a Daughter, You Are This Kind of Beautiful," "Wishes for You, Daughter," "Have Some Fun!," "Daughter, You Are Such a Blessing to Me," and "You've Earned Your Wings... Fly!" Copyright © 1997, 1999, 2000, 2001 by PrimaDonna Entertainment Corp. All rights reserved.

Barbara Cage for "Everything I Do as Your Parent, I Do Out of Love for You." Copyright © 2001 by Barbara Cage. All rights reserved.

Barbara J. Hall for "No Matter Where You Go, Daughter, I Will Always Be Here." Copyright © 2001 by Barbara J. Hall. All rights reserved.

Melissa Whitten for "Daughter, Watching You Grow Up Has Been My Life's Reward." Copyright © 2001 by Melissa Whitten. All rights reserved.

A careful effort has been made to trace the ownership of poems used in this anthology in order to obtain permission to reprint copyrighted materials and give proper credit to the copyright owners. If any error or omission has occurred, it is completely inadvertent, and we would like to make corrections in future editions provided that written notification is made to the publisher:

SPS STUDIOS, INC., P.O. Box 4549, Boulder, Colorado 80306.